IMPS

Imps
Mathew V. Spano

*Featuring illustrations
from the works of
Gustave Dore*

Published by **BLAST PRESS**
324B Matawan Avenue
Cliffwood, NJ 07721
(732) 970-8409
gregglory.com

Gustave Dore (1832-1883) was a French artist best known for his wood engraving/printmaking depicting the works of great authors of world literature, such as Dante, Cervantes, Milton, Coleridge, Perrault, and Tennyson.

Copyright © 2018 by Mathew V. Spano

Acknowledgements

The following poems first appeared in:

"A Message from the People of Earth" in *Middlesex: A Literary Journal*, vol. 1, no. 6, 2013.

"Argus" in *Middlesex: A Literary Journal*, vol. 1, no. 7, 2014.

"A Crossing" in *Middlesex: A Literary Journal*, vol. 1, no. 7, 2014.

"House Rules" in *Middlesex: A Literary Journal*, vol. 1, no. 9, 2016.

"Imps" in *Middlesex: A Literary Journal*, vol. 1, no. 7, 2014.

"Jeremiah's Wheel" in *This Broken Shore*, vol. 6, summer, 2013.

"Salamander Brandy" in *Turtle Island Quarterly*, Issue 9, summer/fall 2015.

"Vous etes tous Charlie" in *Psychological Perspectives*, vol. 59, no 1, 2016.

"What Tried To Get In" in *Quantum Fairy Tales*, Issue 14, winter 2016.

"Coyote Alone" in *Psychological Perspectives*, vol. 62, no 1, 2019.

"Scarecrow" in *Psychological Perspectives*, vol. 59, no. 1, 2016.

"Tropical fish tank" in *Frogpond*, vol. 12, no. 2, 1999.

"Extra Innings" in *Modern Haiku*, vol. 36, no. 2, 2005.

"Funhouse Music" in *Simply Haiku*, vol. 5, no. 3, 2007.

"England's Hidden Hops: A Travel Guide" in *Hops, Herb of the Year 2018: Brewing and Beyond*, edited by Gertrude Coleman, The International Herb Society, 2018.

"Canto 33 & 1/3" *Middlesex: A Literary Journal*, vol. 1, no. 5, 2012.

List of Illustrations

Cover Image: Gustave Doré- The Inferno of Dante, 1861

P. 16: Gustave Doré-The Adventures of Baron Munchausen, 1862

P. 26: Gustave Doré-Droll Stories collected from the Abbeys of Touraine by Honoré de Balzac,1855

P. 39: Gustave Doré-Droll Stories collected from the Abbeys of Touraine by Honoré de Balzac,1855

P. 44: Gustave Doré-The Fables of Jean de la Fontaine, 1867

P. 60: Gustave Doré-The Fables of Jean de la Fontaine, 1867

P. 63: Gustave Doré-The Gnarled Monster by Gustave Dore, 1870

P. 72: Gustave Doré-The Adventures of Baron Munchausen, 1862

P. 80: Gustave Doré- The Inferno of Dante, 1861)

P. 85: Gustave Dore-Nouveaux Contes de fées de La Comptesse de Ségur, 1857

P. 90: Gustave Doré-The Adventures of Baron Munchausen, 1862

Contents

A Message from the People of Earth 13
Game Over? 17
Argus 19
Arsenal 21
Backache 22
A Crossing 24
Clean Sweep 25
Crawl Space 27
Dragon 29
House Rules 30
Imps 32
Jeremiah's Wheel? 34
Circus Song of the Monkey Dad 37
Solomon Grundy 40
My Beard 41
Mind Tree 42
Mirror Mirror 45
Off with their heads! 47
Please Pass the Popcorn 48
Pumpkin Pie 49
Salamander Brandy 50
The Word 52
Jesus Surveys Storm Damage 53
The House That God Built 55

Them Apples 57
Vous êtes tous Charlie 58
What Tried to Get In 61
Yin-Yang 64
Ice Fishing 66
Parasite Valentine 68
Manchurian Channidae 70
Pickerel Grin 73
Turtle Soup 74
Katydid Chorus 76
All About Eve, or, Snow White in Reverse 78
Staring Contest with a Giant Pacific Octopus at the Camden Aquarium 81
Coyote Alone 83
Scarecrow 86
Taunt 88
Haiku 91
England's Hidden Hops: A Travel Guide 92
Glenn Gould's 1966 Performance of Beethoven's Pathetique Sonata: A Review in Verse 93
Canto XXXIII (& 1/3) 95

A Message from the People of Earth

"We are trying to survive our time so we may live into yours. We hope some day, having solved the problems we face, to join a community of Galactic Civilizations. This record represents our hope and our determination and our goodwill in a vast and awesome universe."

—Words of President Jimmy Carter inscribed on the Voyager probe launched into space on June 16, 1977.

Who left Puccini
Off Voyager's golden disc?

Tosca's aria
Plunging down to Mars
A rusty dagger thrust
Through Scarpia's ribs.

Gianni Schicchi's Lauretta
Longing for her sweet father...
Raining down
On Jupiter's raging storm.

Butterfly's plaint unwinding,
Threading the asteroid belt,
Slipping through Saturn's rings,
Sighing for Pinkerton's ship
To pierce the dark horizon
With every silent moonrise.

Rodolfo all alone,
Pining for Mimi:
His remorse reaching back
Toward Venus, forever grasping
Empty space and riding
A distant, fading orbit
Around
Cold
Dark
Pluto.

And if there is no one to hear,
No God to bear witness
To our heroic quest,
There is
The adding of a final note:

"Dilegua, o notte!
Tramontate, stelle!
Tramontate, stelle!
All'alba vincerò!

Vincerò!

Vincerò!"

A curse, triumphal, hurled
Into the abyss, the barren forest
Where the lone tree fell.

Game Over?

Asteroid 2015 TB145–
Seven football fields around,
Skull-shaped,
The fathomless orbits
Of its eyes arcing farther,
Now closer, round and round
Every three years
For thirty millennia.

Ymir's great cranium nodding off
Toward Earth; dead comet,
Desiccated angel,
Lucifer's gaze locked on
Target—thieves of Father love,
Cause of his deep-hearted grief
That hurtled him headlong
Into the void, circling.

The rotten grin of Pan Ku, Purusha,
The Great Pumpkin,
Lolling past the open-mouthed moon,
Bowling blindly down the alley
Of the Milky Way
Toward a cosmic strike,

Tunguska kiss times twelve
On Jerusalem or Beijing,
Benares or Bethlehem,
Machu Picchu,
Manhattan or Moscow.

Yahweh yawns,
Tired of having to slap down
These upstart primates,
Makes it a game of chance—
Loves the action, the long odds—
Casts a skull-shaped die our way,
Which we pray will be as Hunter's head,
Bouncing down the long ball court,
Bursting in a shower of pumpkin seeds,
Meteors to illuminate
The long shadows of Xibalba.

Argus

The age, a fallen one.
Down from Olympus, I wander a man,
And the ennui I witness outspans
Even a god's wide gaze.
The people mesmerized—
Their eyes billions of blank screens fixed
On the billions more that flicker and hold them fast.
They sit spellbound by the eyes of Argus,
Forever watching and being watched.
It drives the herds of men, corrals their will,
Pens them in with electric fences
To short circuit contact.
Cut off from caress or the sweet brush of lips,
They forget the feel of rough bark or fine dirt through fingers,
Retreating sands slipping between toes,
The scent of an infant's breath,
The spasm of a struggling trout—-
For these, for everything, they are out of tune.
It moves them not.

How best to strike them blind and open their eyes?
Send Hermes to slip behind a firewall,
Lade the giant's lids with a winsome tune and wink

And hack it in its sleep?
Hurl cyclopean shafts, splinter cell towers,
And rumble belly laughs
As they curse the god-surge?
Flood their waterways—
A many headed hydra for their hydrocarbons?
Will they divine the compassion in my destruction,
Rescue from their own
Promethean thefts?

Arsenal

For all the graduates of Middlesex County College

Ideas undetonated
In minefields of mud
Await the touch of match to fuse,
To arc axon and dendrite
Sparking a Big Bang
Bursting forth in starbursts of verse,
Fountains of formulas.

Out of smoke and shadow,
Neurons crackle,
Synapses hiss.
Mental mortars,
Screech, crackle, boom
In aerial burst—
Chrysanthemum,
Palm Tree,
Willow—
Mind blowing,
Igniting the night.

Backache

The same old carpenter
With a lamb's eyes and a camel's back
Reports promptly each morning at dawn,
Sundays too,
At the site of this crooked old frame
To make repairs.
He walks like he's heading to his own wake,
Descends into the cellar
Where pressure cracks spider web
From the main load-bearing post,
An aging Atlas.

He opens thermos and lunchbox,
Preparing the offering,
The wounds in his workman's hands gaping
Like the holes in his jelly donut bled dry.
Alone, he drags a shoring post and jack
Into position, raising
The house beam, taking on the weight
And strain long enough to take away
The sins of the wood—
Worm-ridden old trunk—
To dig and pour a new footing,
And insert a clean beam, knot-free,
From a young, healthy tree.

Slowly, he lowers the jack,
Slides out the shoring post.
It holds its own for an instant,
Then begins to buckle.
This old house is heavy with junk—
Bad choices piled up
Over a lifetime, all stuffed
Into dark closets and locked chests,
An attic groaning with heaps of guilt,
And the uninvited with *their* baggage,
Some just passing through,
Others squatting for the duration, dumping
Filth too much for even Herakles.

Soon, the new post follows the old,
Fissures in the same places branch
From roots to rafters.
I smile through tears at his failed attempt,
Thankful it's no worse than before,
Knowing he'll be back to try it again.
I beg him to take the rest of the day off:
We'll go to the pub for a pint,
Get drunk and ogle the forbidden fruit,
Then tell dirty jokes about the Architect
With the cruel sense of humor.

A Crossing

Aged lion, he wades half awake
Into a river of traffic, trudging
Toward the annual checkup.
But the Crocodile Time, noting the frayed mane,
Turns in pursuit, overtakes his waning pace.
It locks a gouted heel in jaws of steel,
Bores its bulk into the ruthless surge.
Puffing flame, he kicks harder,
Wide eyes barely cresting the water line.
But in the current of coursing blood,
Something spawned of star stuff stirs:
It grins flashing golden fangs,
Moon eye milky with age,
Sun eye blazing, enraged.
And Time lets go,
Turns tail and drifts away,
Choosing to wait for easier prey.

Clean Sweep

Tattered work clothes cling to the line,
Billow to the late autumn breezes in time.
The wheels of upturned bikes in high grass
Squeal like a pack of ragged black rats.
Weeds force the pavement to buckle and swell,
Buboes bursting up through the skin of Hell.
Hollow-eyed houses gaze up at the sky,
Rows of fresh skulls set out to dry.

No one noticed her baleful lantern appear
In the window of the shack at the edge of the mere.
Her long-fingered shadow reached out, storm cloud
Smothering streetlights beneath a thickening shroud.
The ravens leered down from the bare drooping trees
And cawed the arrival of the dreaded disease.
The harsh whisper of the old woman's broom
Hushed the whole village still as a tomb.
A pity for all those God chose to forsake
She chose the broom instead of the rake.

Crawl Space

Hypnotized,
A boy again seeking lost secrets,
I gaze into this ancient cave
In the bowels of the abandoned house,
A flashlight strobing morphing forms
Of stuffed animals and wind-up beasts
That stir and wait in the black:
Cave bear, saber tooth, wolf pack.

Cave painter
Burrowing back down the birth canal,
I spelunk one last time,
Elbows and knees scraped raw in the scree,
Incense of dust, cobwebs, rot, must;
Shaman summoning spirits of the hunt,
Mammoth, bison, bull,
From the womb of Lascaux or Lespugue.

In the Cave of Hands,
Children's mostly, some mine,
Wave across the gallery of time.
Purple palms sprout
Tiny lifelines; first fingerprints
Spiral down the eons.

Hands by the dozen, traced, painted, decorated:
Some turkeys, others sea stars,
Two together a dove's wings
Opening,
Rainbow butterfly resting on a page,
Reindeer with antlered fingers splayed,
And one offering the sacred gift of an open eye—
All outstretched to grasp
With a final gasp;
They pull me through
To the light I never knew
On the other side.

Dragon

Serpent song summons,
A bite to reach a god,
Tongue piercing flesh, flooding veins,
Deadening senses dead by fire.
What Wyrm stirred deep
When she stumbled down the hole
And glimpsed the glittering hoard
Atop ash and skull, smoldering,
Smoke licking sockets,
Scattered syringes—dragon's teeth—
Spawning skeleton spies
With venom-tipped spears?
From Beowulf's folly, she knows to wait
On Wiglaf, sounds her war horn,
Summons her heroes to stab
Through stubborn scales
And stamp out serpent fire.
They seal the cave and lift the curse,
Planning to cast the coiled carcass
From the sea cliff
Or at least trap beneath Herakles' stone
Its immortal Hydra's head.

House Rules

Dame Fortuna spins her wheel,
A dark Vanna luring Faithful to Vanity Fair.
Beguiled by the prize, we place our bets and let it ride
Like bouncing roulette balls seeking their slots—
Coming up zeroes or cashing it all in.
Will it be the lottery win or the breast lump,
The surgeon's slip-up or the summer chalet,
The plane crash or the promotion?
Rags, riches or both in an endless round?
Cinderella spins and slips on the staircase—
Bippity, Boppety, all bets are off.
The Potter at His wheel makes and unmakes.
Better to heed Buddha and seek the still point
At the center of Samsara's deadly spokes
Off the Karmic carousel.

Dante says the Dame works for the House,
The tough guy in the white tux with a table in the back,
But He's no Rick Blaine, no sage or Sajak,
Plays it too close to the vest,
And never smiles
Because he no longer turns a profit.
His tilted wheel, perhaps, out-rigged,
But how and whose House Rules?

She spins again
With a wink and a nod,
No Garden for this game—a wheel instead, spoked web,
Better suited to her spinning,
And He starts to wonder if she's finally gotten
His number.

Imps

They crouch and leer, bat-faced,
Among the stalactites of gloom,
Waiting to take wing and flutter up
Into the spotlight where, for a flickering instant,
They loom, large as gargoyles.

The urge to giggle in a eulogy;
To refuse to hold your peace forever
And screech some obscene reason why the groom
And the bride should never unite;
The insane itch to French kiss
The boss as she patiently describes
Why your promotion has been denied.
The poltergeist that lets you linger
Holding your wailing infant
Near the bedroom window…open wide to the winter night.
The gremlin perched near the passenger window,
That dares you to veer across the double yellow,
Or the pixie with a needle
Who loves to prick and wheedle you to cut
The headlights down the mountain road,
Just for a second,
Just to see what happens.

They prick with tiny pitchforks,
Make you itch till you swat them like mosquitoes,
Or shoo them away, back to your sewers and caves,
Or stuff them still struggling
Back into your bottle, only to discover
The next time they flutter madly round your lamp
That you forgot to tighten the stopper.

Jeremiah's Wheel?

Left running, the wheel spins on,
The Potter's stool a silent sentinel
To the vessels rising darkly
From wet clay at the hypnotic center
Pulled and shaped by the moon's pale fingers
Into a menagerie of vases, grails, and urns—
Some open-mouthed, waiting to be filled;
Some swan-necked, full-hipped;
Some like the cup of a breast formed to pour;
Some closed tight to seal out all air and light;
Some warped or punctured without purpose or form—

They jostle along a conveyor belt
Into the Hell that hardens them
To receive water, wine, or witch's brew,
Earthenware wombs pregnant with grain,
Ritual tombs for royal ashes,
All nudged onto a splintered shelf
Beneath a dusty bulb that bathes them
For a moment beneath a golden shaft,
A clanking procession that bunches and bulges
Until one by one, or sometimes altogether,
They fall.

Puppet Show (to my future caretakers in the Alzheimer's ward)

Don't be deceived by this mad marionette
That you slap down in a wheelchair,
Strapped in lest the cruel Puppeteer yank on synapses
And send him reeling in a frantic dance,
Then cut the strings to watch him collapse,
Slack limbs fractured,
In a loose pile of kindling.

Don't be deceived by this filthy sock puppet
Flinging curses, foul-mouthed and tattered, forced by a
Fiendish hand
To froth and rage, then clench in a contorted fist
That an exorcist would flee before it's finally released,
Tossed into a hamper in a crumpled heap.

Don't be deceived by this demented dummy
Babbling Biblical riddles from Revelation,
Some vile ventriloquist throwing voices
To the void in the tortured hours of night.

Don't be deceived by the Punch-and-Judy pantomime,
The slapstick shift from sense to violence,
From drug induced drowse to the domestic abuse
That drew his final curtain
And jerked him shrieking to this terminal theater
Of vermin and the absurd.

Instead, listen for the pure soul
That loved and taught and freed so many
From the tangled strings that strangled their fates,
The same soul that casts this voice
Across the decades to you who stand here
Astonished and appalled
Watching this danse macabre,
Wondering if this perverse
Pinocchio-in-reverse
Was ever a real live boy.

Circus Song of the Monkey Dad

Tiger Mom cracks her whip!
Five cubs bolt upright at attention—
All in a row, rows of neat teeth,
Rarely bared, constantly clenched,
Tongues wrapped tight,
Claws sheathed for the choreographed show.
They trot in tight circles, leap through hoops of flame,
Barrel walk, dance a minuet to her monotone—
Whipped to submit, tamed to perfection.
She lords their mastery
Over us slovenly spectators—obese apes with bratty monkeys,
Blank gazes, mouths agape, never bothering to wipe
Noses that slowly dribble into dripping ice cream cones.

But when the lights come up and the applause fades,
I slip my five little monkeys into the shadowy sideshow
(No place for tiger cubs!)
Where they dare to enter the lair
Of the Alligator Man! Gasp
At the menacing grasp of the Lobster Lady! Weep
At the pathos of Wolf Boy and Camel Girl! Behold
The Wild Man of Borneo! Gawk

At the abomination of the Elephant Man, and marvel
At the Human Owl, Fiji Mermaid,
The Ostrich People of Zimbabwe!
My five little monkeys, moon-eyed, stroke the bally stage—
Their Monolith—
Imaginations uncaged, soaring
Like trapeze stars, swallowing flaming swords
Of radical amazement, taking fire
Into the belly.
Bantum Barnums,
They will seek out the Geek Shows, peek
Beneath tent flaps, find the seams between
The rings, and never, ever,
Jump through hoops of flame.

Solomon Grundy

Solomon Grundy
Resurrected on Sunday,
Worshipped on Monday,
In the tabloids by Tuesday—
Betrayed on Wednesday,
Tried on a Thursday
Then flogged on Friday—
His stoning on Saturday,
Cremation on Sunday:
Truly the end
Of Solomon Grundy.

My Beard

May my beard continue to bloom long after I'm gone.
Buried in an oblong pod
Of burnished oak or pine,
I give it leave to shoot forth hairy filaments, fibrous feelers,
Probe for crannies, tiny cracks that hide in the hinges of
    a coffin lid,
Pry open a sliver just wide enough
For sprouting finger and toenails to curl & twine like
tendrils Of an iron vine punching through
    concrete slabs,
Mingle with mycelia, hoary rhizomes and wildflower roots,
Groping for the first pale glint
Of snow-filtered sun.

Mind Tree

With the first leaves, a few years fall—
He's teaching once again the alchemy
Of carbon rings and serpents
That bite their own tails
To wide-eyed acolytes,
Transmuting lead into gold.

With the first nuts to fall,
Six decades drop away,
And he crawls once again
Through Korean mud
Dragging back blackened corpses
Through slippery blood
To bury like acorns
That he still has faith will sprout.

A wave of leaves and nuts
Blot the sky like Black Tuesday—
He's a boy hawking old newspapers,
Stuffing them down shoes and sleeves
To feed the embers of his dreams.

In the quickening storm
A stiff limb fractures and falls,
Lights flicker, and he feels medieval.
The Black Death is at the door:
A barricade of tables and chairs,
Scissors crammed into every crevice
To sever skeletal fingers that try to pick
The padlocked fontanels
And raid the cranial vault.

A wild gale shatters
The biggest branches—bringing him
All the way back to protect the pack:
Alpha male hackles raised,
Eyes like ice picks, fangs forward
To greet all challengers with a savage grin.

Lightning strike splits
The trunk down to the core,
Stripping him down to the reptile—crocodile
That lies in wait as though paralyzed
For a limb to stray too close
Then lashing out in hunger and fear—
To survive!
To survive!
To survive!

A final storm blast
Uproots the oak—it lies toppled,

Alone among the survivors that sway,
Sigh and stare down, gathered around.
Its essence laid bare
Roots to nuts, lived through utterly,
Silent in the sudden shafts of sunlight
And the return of birdsong.

Mirror Mirror

"Carrasco cured Quixote,"
Teachers enlighten students
While mothers advise daughters,
"Alice dreamed Hatta
And Grimhilde devoured Snow White."
"Respectable clothing makes character
And Daedalus freed Icarus,"
Fathers coach sons
As elders guide grandchildren,
"Magic isn't real,
Ants over grasshoppers."

"Reality over dream," reveal adults to
Children
To adults reveal," dream over reality."

"Grasshoppers over ants,
Real isn't magic,"
Grandchildren guide elders
As sons coach fathers,
"Icarus freed Daedalus
And character makes clothing respectable."

"White snow devoured Grimhilde and
Hatta dreamed Alice,"
Daughters advise mothers
While students enlighten teachers,
"Quixote cured Carrasco."

Off with their heads!

(for Alan Henning)

Both with a British dialect—
The one kneeling, robed in red,
Wearing a martyr's heart,
The other erect, locked in black,
Bedeviled to behead.
Surely switched at birth—
The one sweetly suckled
By that heroic mother of Horus,
Who made her husband whole,
And wanders, gathering severed parts,
The ragged and the wrathful,
To her fragrant breast.
The other reared by that heartless queen,
Harvester of heads, shrieking sentences
Sans all sense of justice.
If only we could 'waken her wise husband,
Noble King of Hearts,
Whose gentle brush along her arm
Might calm her wild gaze
With a dark and sullen look
From a lost and frightened child.
If only we could murder time,
Stay the sentence, cop a plea...
Until Alice arrives for tea.

Please Pass the Popcorn

The Dead must pity us,
Mourn us as they long to whisper
A faint "Hello" through the dusty panes
Of black framed portraits looming
In our living rooms.
They long to step out from behind a mirror
To straighten a necktie or tighten a corset,
To warn us of a gathering storm
Or listen to our petty fears with smiling eyes
And knowing nods.
They watch us on TV, raising their remotes,
Shouting "Look out for the waterfall!"
Even as we row harder with the current
Racing over rapids deepening downstream.
Most of all, they wish we could watch
Right alongside them,
Laugh and cry all the while
Remembering to pass the popcorn.

Pumpkin Pie

Peter, Peter Pumpkin Eater,
Had a wife he thought a cheater.
He locked her in his pumpkin shell
Which turned into her padded cell.

Peter, Peter Pumpkin Eater,
Trapped another and used to beat her,
But when it came to do or die,
She minced him into pumpkin pie!

Peter, Peter Pumpkin Pie,
No longer makes his women cry.
From her shell each one emerged
And on dessert they all converged!

Salamander Brandy

Catch three live ones, clever theft
Of red efts, steaming beneath the dead leaf heap,
Drop them into a barrel of burning blackberries
Until they secrete their secret spell
And the magic tragic poison potion
Goes down warm and smooth in the autumn glow.
Golden dewdrops tap eyelids open
To a garden humming with mushrooms,
Devil's Urns, spewing a spore-cloud
From which suddenly darts a giant garter,
Toxin taster; he gathers you in by inches,
Pulling relentlessly into his serpent's black belly.
You learn to live by candlelight and playing cards,
Which you ignite to send smoke signals
To a waiting army of gnomes who swarm
The glutted giant, surgically slicing
The reptile gut with tiny swords,
Resurrection via c-section—all except
Hands and wrists, left as payment
To the great snake.

Let another sip slither past your parted lips
And sprout a thousand new limbs—
Arms fanning in a halo of hands,
Each palming a single eye peering deep

Into the roots of diseased trees,
Trunk hollows twisted in silent screams.
Until the shrews show up nosing a meal,
Nipping with needle teeth to bleed a dream,
But you let drop a thousand tails that writhe and scurry
Luring the malevolent moles
Who hurry after down dark holes filled with black pitch.

Now you are free—finally free
To crawl through funeral fires into the sunrise
To be baptized by the Emperor of India.

The Word

The word

Unfurls

Little by little,

A new rose,

Open to the world,

Loosening its darkness,

Blind to the hailstorm,

Leaning into light.

Jesus Surveys Storm Damage

Watching footprints fade
In Red Sea sand,
Jesus decides to end
His lost years, divines his calling
Along a self-guided tour
Of storm-ravaged lands
In the hurricane wake
Of Yahweh's wrath.
In loose sand sifting
Through open fingers,
He feels the final fear
Of the Egyptian charioteer
Who was just following the orders
Of Pharoah
Who was just following orders
Of heart-hardening Yahweh.

He likewise sifted the sands
That once packed the walls
Of Jericho and stacked the frame
Of the Canaanite whore,
Informant to Joshua
Whose horns bellowed

The wall-tumbling war whoop
Of heart-hardening Yahweh
With His merciless *herem*.
And he wrote songs of mercy
For the sins of the sons
And daughters of Sodom
In fertile sands that once played
Across the city Abraham tried to spare.

He is haunted by the cries
Of Pharoah's first-born
In the sirocco passing over,
The elegy of the innocent
Who would not be passed over
By heart-hardened Yahweh.

The House That God Built

These are the Bacteria

> that God built.

These are the Algae and Amoebae

> that God built.

These are the Worms, Fish, Frogs

> that God built.

These are the Lizards, Rats, Apes

> that God built.

These are the People

> that God built.

These are the Vaccines

                      that God built

For the People to kill the Bacteria

                      that God built.

Them Apples

Serpent:

Why take just one bite,
From just one apple,
From just the one tree,
When you could pluck the other,
A sweet Golden,
Taste,
And live in eternity?

Eve:

Having bitten the bitter fruit,
We lost all taste for the sweet.
With knowledge, death is born,
And only in innocence
Can we live forever.
Our bellies full,
Now we hunger
For new fruits:
We two the only trees
Blossoming,
Intertwined,
In our own eternity.

Vous êtes tous Charlie

Prometheus crucified to a crag;
Monkey locked in a crucible and cooked;
Loki enduring the venom drip
From the viper's fang;
Raven all singed, tail feathers trailing
Plumes of smoke;
Bre'r Rabbit itching for a fight,
Stuck tight in pitch;
Bugs holed up in his bunker,
Ducking Elmer's double-barrel;
Voltaire honing his quill
By a dying lantern
In the bowels of the Bastille;
Salman scrambling
To the next safe house, scribbling
Madness in the pale moonlight.
Scheherezade stretching out her yarn
Beyond first light; hoping to embrace
Another day;
Rénard reclining in his coffin,
Slight smile fixed
On pursed fox lips.

Vous êtes tous Charlie.
Though always in a bind,
You find a way to rise,
Bring us fire and light,
Pull down our pants,
Strike up the phallic parade.

Through you, we laugh at our lapses,
Weep at our weakness,
Cringe at our cruelty.
You satirize the senate,
Parody the priests.
You x-ray our offenses,
Expose our two faces,
Incite against injustice,
Ignite to revolution.

You burn us down
So we can sprout anew.
Satyr, fool, jester,
Comedian and quester,
Catalyst and questioner—
Trickster *pour toujours,*
La liberté au delà de la mort.

What Tried to Get In

After a wild night of wind and lightning,
My wife, wide-eyed in the ragged moonlight,
Awakens to my hoarse whisper and anxious claim
Of something large clambering across the gabled roof—
What sounds to me like the gnawing of rafters
By hooked teeth and jagged claws.
Dismissing my hunch with a sigh and a yawn,
She waves me back to bed
Convinced a nightmare must have galloped
Through my sleep and lingers still
Insatiate, just outside the stable gate.

But whatever landed with a thud a moment ago
Likely sniffs out the loose seams in the shingles
To pry a portal large enough
To slip through with folded wings
And retractable talons—
Some wretched Grendel
Dropping like a fallen gargoyle,
Dead to reason, bent on stuffing our young
Into his great scaly purse bulging with the bones
Of neighborhood kids whose parents somehow
Didn't sleep lightly enough.
A shape-shifter perhaps, slithering

Through vents and shafts,
Puffing dream dust into our eyes to set them spinning,
Hell bent on bolting down bone and brain
While we doze disarmed, warm near the hearth
Of our own private Heorot.

My menacing knocks on the ceiling,
Convey my meaning: Morse Code via Louisville Slugger,
Give this bugger pause to prick up pointed ears
And listen long for me listening for him
In the leaden silence—
Each of us plotting the other's next move
Till, perhaps preferring easier pickings,
He surely lifts off into the gloom of the half moon
No trace by daylight of his intended invasion, save the gutter—
Utterly bent, no doubt, by debris brought down
By the howling storm—bulky broken boughs
That are somehow now nowhere to be found.

Yin-Yang

Flytrap flashes Venus,
Flaunts rose lobes,
Locks twitching wings
With a spring loaded kiss.
Locust flashes, swarms,
Strips yielding leaves,
Rapes valleys bare.
Sundew unfurls
Lithe sequined limbs
In early light,
Fixes fast the lusty bee
In an embalmer's embrace.
Weevil seeds pregnant ears
With legions of leeching worms.
Fairy bells summon toddlers,
Turn to witches' thimbles
That lodge in soft throats.

Spin the boardwalk wheel,
Bet on black or white,
It matters not—the game plays on
With no end in sight.
But far out at sea,
Up from the dark,

A luminous sea slug glides in silence,
Sipping genes from algae fields,
So much green tea,
Finds the depth where light likes to hide,
Thrives on the sun in the shadowy tide.

Ice Fishing

Auger down
Through six inches
Of stockade ceiling
Liquid life locked down
Barred from the icy light,
The seething deep
Teeming
With Viking violence.

Drop braided lines
Baited with scraps
Of yesterday's feast—
A stew of rotten grudges,
Heaps of treacherous urges,
Clumps of jealous surges,
Swallowed whole through
Sleet-crusted beards,
Down mouths that ice over fast
Forming the frozen surfaces
Of fellow men's kindly faces,
Yielding no sign besides
Their frigid grins locked tight
Like smiling pike.

The tip-ups tell it's time
To pull up from this Nordic moor
Umbilical cords laden with deadfall.
But something's alive on number four—
Beware as you reach down
the slushy hole; you may have just hooked
The Midgard Serpent caught by Thor
Before he cut the line,
Fearing the world's end.

Parasite Valentine

Three cheers for the chiggers!
Let's hear it for the head lice!
Give it up for giardia!
Though you're sometimes found
Face-down in feces,
Every host knows
You're the secret life of the party!
You get things moving, mingling blood
Of illicit lovers, like Donne's flea,
Picking fights with lymphocytes,
Unblocking clots of party poopers!

Granted, you don't know when to quit,
Call it a night, make a grand exit.
You hang on like a hookworm for days and weeks,
Stealing everyone's meals, eating all the snacks,
Depleting the toilet paper,
Taking the good pillows
Like bedbugs moving in for a feast.
You subvert the servants, lay the maids
Like Penelope's suitors,
Feed on brains, amoeba zombie looters.

But, truth to tell, you also weaken prey,
Prime our immunity,
Make off with heavy metals,
Heal without impunity.
With the hidden bite of a wood tick,
You smuggle in the good stuff
Numb overactive nerves
So we never feel the needle prick.
And if we survive your boorish stay,
Perhaps we'll crash YOUR party one day,
Stay long after it's over,
Leech out your mystery,
Take you back,
A chastened lover.

Manchurian Channidae

"Channa argus (the northern snakehead)
Is the kindest,
Gentlest,
Most unobtrusive
Fish I've ever studied,"
Proclaimed the fishery official at the DNR.
But we anglers know you swim among us,
Aquatic assassin in a slime-dark trench coat,
More serpent than SEAL, outfitted
By evolution with Q-gadgets galore, gulping
Air through a hidden lung ("labyrinth organ"),
Scaly snake face concealing the ravenous scowl
With a dagger-ridged kiss.
You wriggled your way through the underworld
From China, North Korea, and Russia (with love),
Stealth landing behind a non-descript strip mall
In a Crofton pond concealed
Like the Creature From the Black Lagoon—
You lay in wait for heavy rain and runoff.
Serpent spy, sliding at night on elbows and belly
Through wet grass and brush,
Backyard and barbed wire,
From pond to stream,
Stream to river, under cover

Of mud and flood, dodging
Pesticide and poison, electrofishing
And ranks of angry anglers
Unleashing volleys of barbed steel,
Up the Potomac to the tidal basin—
Within slithering distance of the White House,
Overpowering, out-devouring the native bass
To make sure you're the one that ends up
On the President's line.

Pickerel Grin

The pickerel I lured from the shrouded canal
Had the grin of a Murphy or Hoolihan—twisted smile
Of all who dug by hand the sixty-six miles,
Their bleached bones dumped in an unmarked hole,
Their souls leaching into the leaden current.

Defiant underbite, lips drawn tight,
Exposing his jagged grin: the wild-eyed grimace
That follows sharp despair when told
Of the dollar-a-day wage for toil
In a self-dug grave—the cholera,
Shredded hands and feet, bloody rags
For shoes—tattered fins that flail
Against the current; thinly veiled rage
At having to stomach his terms to heed
The starving screams of the suckling overseas.

The hook set, he thrashes his chains
Against the bars of the net.
I'll flay him and set free his watery ghost,
Make of him a communion meal: raise a Host,
Eat of his flesh, drink sacred wine,
And swallow the soul of all his suffering.

Turtle Soup

Made with alligator snapper—the appetizer
Opening the awards banquet.
But his life force lingers still
In the heavy brown broth.
A molten spoonful draws
Me down the bowl's swirling
Mud hole, his cold blood slowly flooding
The chambers of my heart.

Something digs in
Against your admonishing glances,
Gazes up at your gossips like goslings
That have strayed into dangerous waters,
Glares at your polite assembly—speeches sputtering
On the surface, platitudes plashing
Like fatigued frogs teasing a hair trigger spring,
A trap loaded to snap up the whispers and quips
That dart around the table like minnows lured
To my murky den with a twitch of worm tongue—
I wait, an angler from the abyss.

Lure me out at your peril, I'll not budge:
My long clawed gauntlets bore into bedrock
Beneath sand and silt where I lodge and seethe—

An anvil in Vulcan's forge.
Spiked tail protruding from heavy armor,
Some dark magic must have merged in me
Black knight with black dragon.

Wait me out?
I'll winter six months plus without a breath,
Gnawing on a grudge like Ugolino
Beneath Cocytus' stinking ice.
Your thaw only stokes my appetite,
And the eye of my vice looks to lock on a target—
The fingers of your outstretched hand?—
For my steel beak to neatly cleave.

Dispatch your envoys, cygnets
Paddling heedlessly, dangling
Their delicate feet over my dungeon—
I'll snap them down one at a time leaving
Just the snowflake down dancing
On the settling surface.

Katydid Chorus

A secret society
Of snitching schoolgirls,
Antennae twice their body size,
All abuzz on a summer eve
With the news, the burning news,
Ignited from dried thighs
Rubbing together,
That *she did it*—
Burst a precious vase,
Shattered virgin crystal,
Then lied to her loving parents.
Their cliques all a-clicking, all atwitter
Along their insect net.

A coven of hissing crones
Perched in barren branches,
Who testify *she did it*—
Stole from the church basket
To feed her bastard son—
Who boast they'll strike her down
With a bolt from the black,
New-moon sky.

A jury of gossips,
Whispering guilt or innocence,
Deliberating,
Dropping rumor from the eaves
Of the inn, the false claim
She did it—
Poisoned the newlyweds
In a jealous fit.

A summons
For the killing frost.
Their whispers razors
Endlessly scraping the strop.
Their mandibles
Able to pierce even the warm flesh
Of tiny mammals.

All About Eve, or, Snow White in Reverse

Imagine Snow White sucked down
The black blood of the wicked queen
When she sank her perfect, pointed pearly whites
Into that poisoned, heart-shaped apple—
Got a taste
Of power and ambition,
Swallowed the old witch's cunning and craft,
Along with her flair for the dramatic—
But kept the alabaster complexion,
Chill beauty of the bloodless.

Imagine the wicked queen
Naïve of what she just gave away,
Losing her magic along with her memory
(The withering fruits of age),
Suddenly sorry for the pure peasant girl
With the talent show sob story—
Mother's death, father's absence,
Psychotic stepmother's attempts on her life,
Abducted and enslaved to strange little men
Out in the deep woods.

And the magic mirror missing—
Stolen in fact by the little vamp—
And turned now to track
The queen wherever she tries to hide,
Even to her dressing room after the last curtain call,
To betray the spider veins behind the beauty mask,
The glint of fear in her wide Betty Davis eyes,
The soft spot between the neck's deepening creases,
That makes her salivate.
But the mirror shows nothing
When *she* asks the infamous question—
She's forgotten what they say
About vampires and mirrors—
And the tailor's mirror shows no more,
Only emptiness—voids within voids—
In the wells of her soul and the souls of all
Who taste the poison apple.

Staring Contest with a Giant Pacific Octopus at the Camden Aquarium

Sucked in by your hypnotic gaze,
I calcify and drown in your coral maze.
With eight you radiate from Medusa's head
Luring men to your den of the dead.

Carnivorous placental,
Poison thorn with flowing tendrils.
You wait within your vaginal lair
Eyes narrowed in a seductive glare,
Scheming through suctioned tentacles,
Scylla's constricting umbilicals.

You size up patrons with a hooker's leer—
You'd tap a shoulder, disappear,
Pick a pocket, snatch a purse,
Your head the breast of a murderous nurse.
You'd seize a child, slip through bars,
Emasculate security guards,
Dismantle filters, scale glass walls,
Pick all the locks down aquarium halls,
Devour damselfish without a trace,

Lure divers to a Kraken's embrace.
You'd jettison a limb for misdirection,
Ink a shroud to avoid detection.
Jet the scene cloaked in coral—
Hecate who-dunnit without a moral.

But I finally break your Gorgon stare,
Disentangle from your coiled hair,
Glimpse your visage in aquarium glass,
Athena's shield of burnished brass,
Don Hades' stealthy crown,
In the shimmering shadows stand my ground,
Unsheathe Zeus's killing gift,
My father's ancestral blade I lift.
Unlike Oedipus having slain the Sphinx
Just to be devoured in her cunning jinx,
With harpe sword I deal decapitation
Before you complete your Calypso castration.

Coyote Alone

Before Easter, it incarnates
Out of mangy morning smog,
Lopes through manicured lawns,
Bolts across Main Street.
Stuns rush hour traffic
To a screeching standstill.
Strikes smart phones dumb
All eyes on hunched hackles,
Bleeding lips curled
Over gleaming canines.
Bears down on children
At the bus stop frozen
Like lawn deer—
Locks up their limbs,
Loosens bladders.
They await the sharp snap at the nape,
The quick twist, and life dripping
With the runoff down storm drains.

Corners left at the last second,
Down a side street,
Through their backyards,
Toward the river,
Perhaps to die.
Runs fast on just three legs,

Right forelimb dangling,
Nearly severed by an SUV moments before—
A Road Runner running late,
Whose "Beep! Beep!" did not equate
In the beast's Apex brain.
It saw a metal monster
With hard armor, not fur,
Deadlight eyes, and grillwork fangs
That swallowed blacktop and spit gravel.
It felt the black claws that grind bone and fur.

Now, relies on all his wiles,
To make it back alive to the den
Where wife and pups await a kill.
Lumbers limping
Through polished swing sets in the shadow
Of new McMansions,
Where swingers swap spouses
And wolf packs attack each other,
While the sheep safely graze.
The children stand stunned
By the quick change
From beast to victim,
The trickster tricked,
A stumbling Steppenwolf,
His near-severed limb swinging
Like a pendulum
Through their nightmares.

Scarecrow

He hangs, a husk
On a wooden cross
Beneath the rusted windmill and empty silo
On a hill outside of town—
The only cornfield left, a patch
Ripped from a generation past,
Antique ornament for the new pox
Of pressboard mansions on electric green lots.

Children pause to mock him
As they cut through his kingdom unchecked
In their daily pilgrimage from school to screen.
They taunt him to come down from his cross
And play a while in the twilight
And tweet his image with hashtag jokes
And leave plastic bottles and spent syringes at his shrine.

Tonight he will rise
With the harvest moon, blood moon,
To slash tires with a rusted scythe,
Sweeten diesel tanks with sugar
To silence bulldozer and backhoe,
Snatch up logging stakes and spike sycamores,
Cut phone cables and fell cell trees,
Fracture foundations and torch trailers.

But all the children will see the next day
Is the same boney frame draped
In tattered flannel, moldy hat atop
A burlap sack with black hole sockets
That suck their souls
And a jagged mouth, loosely stitched with old shoelaces
Undone a little more than the day before
In what might be called Earth's grimace
Or her gaping grin.

Taunt

How did you feel
When we murdered your Mother?
Raped her first,
Then left her for dead?
Did you know we'd pumped
Her full of our pills—
Dumped birth-control,
Anti-depressants, opiates—
Defiled her amniotic current
With our vile spills?
Did you know
She'd morph into a monster,
Churning a witch's brew
In her toxic womb?

What did you think
When you snagged the body
Of her child and dragged it writhing
From the tainted birth canal—
Horrific half-brother,
Mutated fish,
Cyclops eye dangling
Over a mangled maw,
Another hydra head sprouting

From its flank—
Like Gaia birthing
The hundred-handed ones?

So what did you think
When we murdered your Mother?
And more important—
What are you going to do about it?

Haiku

tropical fish tank—
fingerprint smudges
on the "Do Not Touch!" sign

extra innings—
the vendor sips
his own beer

fun house music
the pretty vendor flashes
her tongue stud

first noble truth:
a hooked trout dangles
from a branch

England's Hidden Hops: A Travel Guide

For the more adventurous,
The *Slaughtered Lamb* pub lies
Shrouded in mist among the moors,
Tucked in a lone grove of weeping willows
Slowly being strangled by the "Willow Wolf"—
Hops bine *Humulus lupulus*, the secret bitter
In its famous *Howl n' Bay* IPA
(A potent Bavarian hops first harvested
By Hildegard of Bingen, pub dwellers tell,
Springing from her vision of The Five Beasts—
The Grey Wolf proclaiming the end of days).
Groggy patrons can take a room upstairs
For the night, drowse deep on a dream pillow
Filled with old Hildy's hops
And drift across the moon-hazed moors
Of sleep, their disturbed dreams bleeding
Into baleful waking daze.

Glenn Gould's 1966 Performance of Beethoven's Pathetique Sonata: A Review in Verse

With the opening chords, we plod aboard
Our Pequod—would-be whalers, landlubbers
Curious about the rumors of the Hell-bent captain,
That virtuoso of ivory, Physeter Faust.
To the thud of his jawbone trudge,
The heavy gait of Fate, we clear moorings,
plotting a course to perdition.
With the first cascading run, we plunge
From the davits—his harpoon planted, we scud
The surface, seat rows turned whaleboats!
The keys of the white concert grand keen
Into whale teeth, the open lid yawns
Wider, revealing ravaged wrecks
And bleached bones of those drowned souls
Foolish enough to haul cables and hoist sails
Seeking the new whale road,
Swallowed whole in the first movement's whirlpool.

Our Ahab embraces the *Gravé*,
Hurls curses into the depths, courts the beast
Who obliges with a lightning lunge
By the end of the final run, leaving nothing
But a lone page of sheet music—lifeboat for last notes,
A floating epitaph.

With the *Adagio*, we reach a halcyon dream—
Notes float down like sea birds
Settling on surface wreckage, singing
A prayer for our drowned Ahab,
Who set souls and sails on a beast
He would chase round perdition's flames
Before giving him up. Melody unfurls,
In billowing sails beckoning,
Angelic bark to carry our crew to paradise,
Charting a course to God.

The *Rondo* hauls us back from the gangway
into the maelstrom once again! Our Ahab is alive,
Clawing, stabbing his way out of the Hellish gut!
The sea's heaving contractions
Birth Ahab anew, now Jonah clinging
To a coffin with keys—last lifeboat
Of the proud vessel that made this mad quest.
He leaves us shipwrecked but more alive than before,
Washed up on the alien shore
Of an undiscovered country.

Translation

Canto XXXIII (& 1/3)

(for Dante Alighieri)

CIRCLE NINE: COCYTUS
    Compound Fraud
ROUND THREE: PTOLOMEA
    The Treacherous to Guests
Pedophile Priests
Cardinal Law

Dante and his guide, Virgil, descend through the depths of the Inferno where the sins of treachery are punished; these are the sins of the LEOPARD, which ambushes its prey when it is least suspected. The poets encounter the very worst of these sinners, many of whom are locked within the frozen lake of Cocytus. They slide and stumble to the third round, called PTOLOMEA after Ptolomeus in the book of Maccabees who invited his father-in-law to a banquet and then murdered him there. Ptolomeus, and the others of this circle, have committed the sin of TREACHERY AGAINST HOSPITALITY—that is, they have kindly invited guests to their homes, offering them sanctuary and council, only to exploit their good will and innocence. Dante further learns that this sin is so horrible that it is punished even before death: the sinner's soul flies down to Hell to commence its eternal punishment as a Demon possesses its body while it still lives in the world above. Before leaving Ptolomea, the poets discover an additional ring in the concentric circles of sinners in Cocytus. Here, they discover a special section devoted exclusively to the

PEDOPHILE Priests and those who conspired to cover their serial sexual abuses of children. The priests appear as leopard seals, predators of the Antarctic that prey on baby seals of other related species by ambushing them from beneath the ice. Dante has never seen such a creature, but Virgil, now a shade with divine sight, knows all the creatures on God's earth. The Demons punish these sinners by luring them to the surface and torturing them, just as they lured and abused their innocent victims. The Demons then flay and skin them, revealing naked, kind-faced priests underneath (here, they cannot hide their true predator nature and must wear it on the outside). The priests, in turn, are then skinned by the Demons revealing again the leopard within (in the end, Virgil explains, they are one nature). Dante speaks to one CARDINAL LAW, a sinner who conspired to cover up the priests' predation.

Reader, forgive me if in my haste
I failed to tell of a sin so cold
It could only be punished in that waste

Where those who betrayed human warmth and trust
And preyed on the pure and innocent lie
Locked in the icy lake of Cocytus.

Perhaps I, like you, didn't care to hear
In the howling winds children wailing
As though crouched behind a wall in fear.

"Master, what is this desolate tract
And why is it here?" My guide replied grimly,
"This ice conceals a terrible fact:

The waters beneath are fed by the spring
Of all the tears shed by innocents,
That freeze when they reach this remote ring.

Hidden deep lurk predators with kind smiles,
"Good Shepherds" who feed on innocent lambs,
As Leopard Seals on pups—the priest pedophiles."

To me such beasts from the opposite pole
Were alien, but my master knew all
Of God's creatures, even those without souls .

Through the frozen haze my master compelled
Me to spy a troop of demons, who,
Instead of pitchforks in hairy claws held

Jagged harpoons, clubs and steel augurs
And a small pen of seal pups just stripped
From their dams, forlorn and beleaguered.

The demons paired off: one drilled a hole
Down through the ice, and one tied a leash
To the trembling pup's neck—its sole

Chance for survival from the attack
To come from below. It wailed for its ma,
The demons' clubs behind their winged backs.

Then, it rocketed up through the ice,
A fanged sea beast—all spotted and sleek—
Man turned to monster, exposing its vice.

It lunged forward toward the pup's bleating,
Its black lifeless eyes filled with hunger,
Its huge maw wide, the pup retreating.

But before it reached the paralyzed babe,
The demons quickly yanked it away,
Then harpooned the beast as it cursed and raved.

"The nature of these fiends" my master told,
"is to prey on the pups, ambushing them,
Then pray for their victims to save their souls."

I saw what he meant in the collars of priests,
Worn around the sleek necks of the monsters,
By which the demons hauled up the beasts

Onto the ice where they skinned them alive,
Defanged them and with circumcision knives
Left them for dead, of their manhood deprived.

And then, Reader, imagine my fright,
When inside that leopard skin was revealed
A kind-faced young priest, all naked and white.

"Here, they wear their true natures outside,
The inverse of their kind natures above
That concealed the predator inside.

But don't be deceived," he went on to say,
"in the end they are but one nature."
The demons then proceeded to flay

And skin the kindly priest and from inside
Emerged a leopard seal, vile as before:
It dove back down the icy hole to hide.

"Worse than Ugolino!" I cursed him, appalled,
"who, starving himself, ate his starved children,
But you, Father, plied yours with Peter and Paul!"

At the next hole down, however, a man
Not a beast had been caught and was questioned
By several more of that troop of the damned.

"Yes," my guide replied before I could ask,
"go question him and learn what treachery
He made for years with his holy mask."

The sinner recoiled as I drew near
And shivered from fear as much as from cold
Dreading the tale he must both tell and hear.

"I elected popes," he puffed up his pride,
Despite standing naked in the ice
"and at one's funeral did I preside.

I dwell now among the damned as you see,
For feeding these beasts and covering tracks,
For this I pay for all eternity."

No sooner did he complete his thought
When he tried to jump back down the hole
In the ice through which he was first caught

But three gaffs did his attempt frustrate
The demons bound him with thick fishing line
And dangled him down the hole as bait.

"Would you like to confess? Care to atone?"
The demons mocked. "Here! Instead of that cross
Around your neck try wearing this millstone!"

"No need to fret!" as he sank fast I cried,
"There is no cause for concern—these leopards
Are quite tame—it's their *victims* who lied!"

At this insult my master rejoiced,
Hugging me close and slapping my back,
"Yes!" he shouted, "you have made a wise choice!"

But he stopped his praise when he caught sight
Of my troubled expression: "My son,
What darkness now can I bring to light?"

"Master, that sinner hasn't yet died;
Cardinal Law still lives. Why has his soul
With Minos' coils already been tried?"

Then my master heaved a heavy sigh
As one who must relay a painful truth:
"This sin is so vile we don't wait till they die.

Their souls fly to Hell leaving behind
Their bodies to be filled by Demons
Who consecrate the host and the wine."

I wept for the children, victims of lies,
In Hell on Earth, but my master replied:
"Grieve not: this day they play in Paradise."

Thinking of this, I kissed my crucifix
And braced for the rest of grim Cocytus.

About the Author

Mathew V. Spano has published poetry, short stories, and essays over the last twenty-five years, many of which are included in his first book *Hellgrammite* (BLAST Press, 2016). His work has appeared in various publications, such as *The Los Angeles Times, Psychological Perspectives, Turtle Island Quarterly, Quantum Fairy Tales, The Yellow Chair Review, Frogpond, Cicada, This Broken Shore, The Heron's Nest,* and *Middlesex*, as well as in anthologies, such as *Palisades, Parkways & Pinelands* (Blast Press, 2016); *Baseball Haiku: The Best Haiku Ever Written About the Game* (W.W. Norton & Co., 2007); and *The Poets of New Jersey: From Colonial to Contemporary* (Jersey Shore Publications, 2005). He has taught English Composition and Mythology in Literature as a full-time professor for over twenty-five years at Middlesex County College in Edison, NJ where he now serves as the English Dept. Chair. He earned his Ph.D. in

Comparative Literature from Rutgers University in New Brunswick, NJ, his dissertation focusing on the works of pioneering psychologist Carl Jung and Nobel laureate Hermann Hesse. Mat lives with his wife Stephanie and their two children in central NJ.

Whys & Wherefores

Meet Me in Botswana: What Is Blast Press?

A speech for national poetry month about BLAST PRESS.

Ab li dolen in l'air [look up: beauty falls from the air]
"A book should be a ball of light in your hands."
~~Ezra Pound

As we all know, April is "International Guitar Month." But my heart twangs for poetry, and I was invited here to tell you a little bit about a tiny poetry publishing company called **BLAST PRESS**.

Description of BLAST PRESS

BLAST PRESS is what I would call a "micro-publisher." We usually publish chapbooks—booklets under 100 pages in length. Our print runs are usually under 100 copies per edition. And **BLAST PRESS** has published over 100 chapbooks from some 20 authors in its career. The entire cost is assumed by **BLAST PRESS**, so we are the publisher, and not a vanity press or service.

BLAST PRESS has been sustaining its small operation—in the black, mind you, no small feat—for about 20 years now. We have had a few more ambitious titles where the book itself, the author, and **BLAST PRESS** decide to dedicate the extra resources needed to make the event a success.

Part of the **BLAST PRESS** ethos is to keep the authors in charge of their work so that they can maintain maximum control of their creative material in the outlying years and don't need to be writing to **BLAST PRESS** for permission to re-publish snippets or poems.

BLAST PRESS
324B Matawan Avenue
Cliffwood, NJ 07721
(732) 970-8409
gregglory.com

Our Credo
Do not dispraise the light
That, singing whatever's brightest,
Undoes the theft of night—
—Touch to caress, or move to love,
As this thoughtless rhyme does prove.
   From **Ascent**

A Solitary Headstone

Niggling addendum to "Meet me in Botswana"

Magazines, published with a week's, month's, quarter's or even a year's date grow elderly on the shelves in a way that a collection of one individual's work never can. What year does Shakespeare's book expire? Horace is renewed year by year, no matter how worn his saws may wane. But a magazine or casual collection of miscellaneous artifacts, no matter how august the individual members of the find, retain an interest for us mostly as a time capsule. Even the Egyptian tombs of the pharaohs hold more interest for us because of what they reveal about the era of their creation than for what they say about their putative occupants. Old poetry quarterlies are no different, although they may contain an Endymion.

This is why **BLAST PRESS** is dedicated to publishing single-author volumes and stand-alone essay collections almost exclusively. Unless a poet is unknown, there is no point in his publication being undertaken by a small press. And if an author is unknown, he is best presented to an unacquainted public in his own exclusive company. It is always wisest to let a guest unroll at least a few of his favorite tales before we escort him from the house. What is characteristic and worthwhile in the poet's voice will quietly assert itself over the course of his varied pieces much better than if we merely heard his alba or evensong in isolation, let alone in the cacophonous squawk of a miscellany. To the marriage of true minds, ours and the author's, let not serial publication admit impediments.

Only appearing in magazines and periodicals is like never having a final resting place—a poet without a plot.

Also Available

Call It Sleep

H. A. Maxson

List Price: $7.75
5.06" x 7.81"
Black & White on Cream
106 pages
SBN-13: 978-0998482927
ISBN-10: 0998482927
BISAC: Poetry / American

About *Call It Sleep*

Call It Sleep contains a final section of poems about a son's experience of a father's illness and death. It give us a snapshot these events in a series of moments, from the onset of the illness to the final moment of death. The book is full of small and large acts of understanding, resonance and respect for one who has gone before. The book touches areas of feeling and experience that confront universal passages of living in a way only very fine poetry can do.

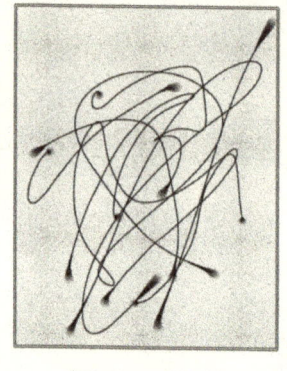

The Giant in the Cradle
Gregg Glory
[Gregg G. Brown]

List Price: $5.50
5.06" x 7.81"
Black & White on Cream
136 pages
ISBN-13: 978-1492396055
ISBN-10:1492396052
BISAC: Poetry / American

FROM THE POEM "HEIGHT OF SUMMER"

Here is the day, the bridal day undaunted;
Here noon, at highest noon... hesitates...
The height of summer, at its crest arrested,
Held between warm hands to kiss—
The levitated real at pause in sun's perfection;
Paused because we cannot see, cannot imagine
Beyond such ripeness—

Yoga Notes
Carrie Pedersen Hudak

List Price: $4.50
5" x 8"
66 pages
ISBN-13: 978-1494330958
ISBN-10: 1494330954
BISAC: Body, Mind & Spirit

From the first essay: Just Practice

When I tell people I am a yoga teacher, they often say, I could never do yoga. I can't even touch my toes. Great, I say, you are already practicing awareness, that's part of the practice. Can you breathe? If you can breathe, then you can do yoga.

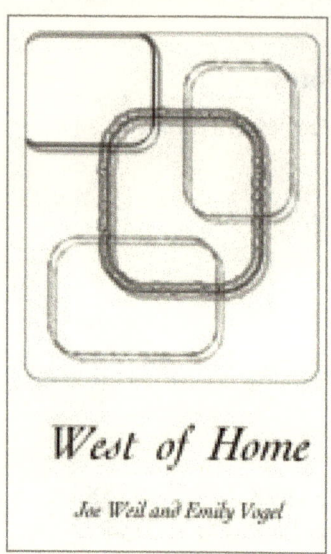

West of Home
Joe Weil, Emily Vogel

List Price: $10.00
Paperback: 98 pages
ISBN-10: 0615878415
ISBN-13:9780615878416
8 x 5 inches

From the Introduction

"West of Home" is a collaborative book of poetry which reflects the present and ongoing sentiments of Joe Weil and Emily Vogel. It includes 14 "responsorial" poems (call and response), between the two poets, as they respond to one another's themes and ideas, as well as two sections of poems, one for each poet's individual work.

Self-Symponies
Daniel Weeks

List Price: $10.00
Paperback: 146 pages
ISBN-10: 0692238581
    ISBN-13:978-0692238585
7.4 x 9.7 inches

From the Introduction

Inspired by listening to the four symphonies of Johannes Brahms, Daniel Weeks's Self-Symphonies explore the landscapes, cityscapes, and seascapes that are the backdrop to a life lived on the New Jersey shore. The four long poems in this collection provide meditations on family, inheritance, and loss, society, nature, and culture, and stasis and change--all of the elements that Coleridge said bething the individual self.

The Pilot Light
Gregg Glory
[Gregg G. Brown]

List Price: $5.50
Paperback: 132 pages
ISBN-13: 9781511941921
5.5 x 8.5 inches

About *The Pilot Light*

The poems in Gregg Glory's The Pilot Light are about relationships—with family, friends, and lovers—along with reminiscences of a childhood spent close to nature in the New Jersey countryside. Glory is particularly adept at exploring the significant and oftentimes intimate moments that define our most important relationships, moments which, in turn, help us create the story of the self.

Knowing the Moment
Emanuel di Pasquale

List Price: $12.95
Paperback: 131 pages
ISBN-13: 9781503117471
5.5 x 8.5 inches

About *Knowing the Moment*

Emanuel di Pasquale has never been one to shy away from the more difficult aspects of living a full and engaged human life, and Knowing the Moment is perhaps his most searing work in this regard, as he confronts the hardships he encountered while growing up in his native Sicily. But these kinds of revelations are never the final word in his poetry. Tough times always seem to point him back to love—as he casts his mind back to life in Sicily or engages with the present in his poems about Long Branch, N.J.

Bee Loud Glade

Authored by
Carrie Pedersen Hudak

Illustrated by
Nuria Tomas Mayolas

List Price: $11.99
Paperback: 36 pages

ISBN-10: 1548983217
ISBN-13: 9781548983215
8.5 x 8.5 inches

About the Bee Loud Glade

A letter from a young woman to her aunt considers printed books and social media.

The Hummingbird's Apprentice

Gregg Glory

[Gregg G. Brown]

List Price: $4.50
Paperback: 159 pages
ISBN-10: 1511941928
ISBN-13: 9781511941921

5.1 x 7.8 inches

From *The Hummingbird's Apprentice*

ROADSIDE WINE

Pull off 71 suddenly, onto
a wide shoulder of dust and grass.
weigh down a length
of brown barbwire fence
like a wave of honey breaking.
Excited, splash ankle-deep
into the unhurrying surf
full of velvety bee sounds, and select
one perfect blossom. It is
so sweet in the slow afternoon.
And, where you've cut your thumb,
a thrill of air catches.

Night, Night
 Gregg Glory
 [Gregg G. Brown]

List Price: $7.75
Paperback: 131 pages
ISBN: 1548801348
ISBN-13: 9781548801342
5.1 x 7.8 inches

From the introduction:

Entering a poem is like entering that other, underwater world. We are restored to a wholeness the pain of life and its deceptions has convinced us is missing. But, we can only hold our breaths so long before our imaginations burst! And still we go down like clockwork into the dark otherwhere of metaphor, easing past the shallow end of simile, our imaginations and lungs aching. However dangerous the journey, we will not be denied our diving, our entry into depths.

American Songbook
Gregg Glory
[Gregg G. Brown]

List Price: $3.75
Paperback: 98 pages
ISBN-10: 1482703297
ISBN-13: 9780692238585
5.5 x 8.5 inches

The Old Truculence

A note concerning the basic arc of this book of poems—to re-register grace and freedom as America's primary metier.

Freedom breeds elegance. Not the inbred elegance of aristocracy, where beautiful ladies eventually come to resemble their Russian wolfhounds. Nor, simply, the truculent elegance of that sly Benjamin Franklin who, as ambassador to the French Court, refused to bow before King Louis the 16th or doff his coonskin cap.

Freedom breeds the desire to create one meaningful action with your entire life—the effortful elegance of the artist that James Joyce defined as the willingness to gamble your whole life on the wrong idea, a bad aesthetic, or, it may be, a genuine triumph. And America has created, and can still create, a unique scale of opportunity for such elegant "throws of the dice," as Mallarme might say. A natty Fred Astaire (originally Austerlitz), gliding with the ease of an ice skater as he backs Rita Hayworth (a gal from Brooklyn) into immortality to a tune penned by the jewish Jerome Kern in an industry patented in the U.S.A. is but one example of the scale of that opportunity.

When you are free to do anything, a desire grows in the breast not to do just anything, but to do the best thing—and that is an aesthetic dilemma. The mere accumulation of capital, or the arbitrary exercise by minor government regulators of petty power, are two classic examples of the desire for a meaningful expression of life-status that lack the aesthetic instinct. Such timid ambitions grow most strongly where the full range of light is narrowed, and the blossom of selfhood must twist around corners to open its ruby glory in a thinning patch of sunlight.

Gregg Glory
March, 2013

Come, My Dreams
Come gather round me, multitudinous dreams
That in the dim twilight are murmuring soft;
Come lay by my head in the pillow-seam;
Come carry my freighted heart aloft.

O, I would dare dream as few men dream
Beyond the cruel cudgel of the strong,
Beyond the purpled tapestries of is and seems
Hung before my eyes, beyond cold right or wrong.

www.ingramcontent.com/pod-product-compliance
Lightning Source LLC
Chambersburg PA
CBHW031401040426
42444CB00005B/374